# JOHN PAUL *Jones*

# *Our* People

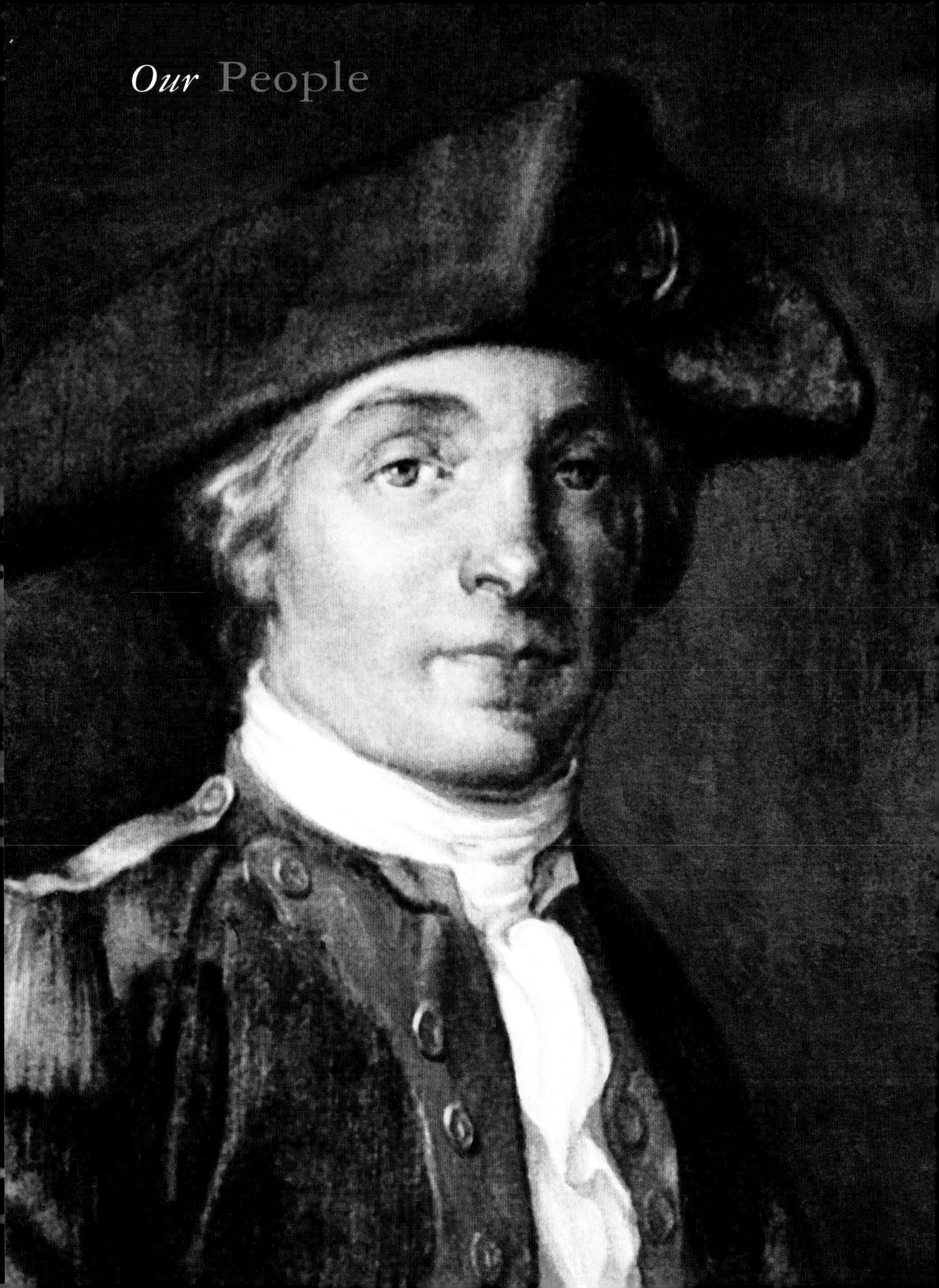

SPIRIT
of America®

JOHN PAUL *Jones*

*By Michael Burgan*

*Content Adviser: Ursula S. Wright, Curator, Portsmouth Historical Society,
Portsmouth, New Hampshire*

*The Child's World®*
*Chanhassen, Minnesota*

6

# JOHN PAUL *Jones*

Published in the United States of America by The Child's World®
PO Box 326 • Chanhassen, MN 55317-0326 • 800-599-READ • www.childsworld.com

*Acknowledgments*

The Child's World®: Mary Berendes, Publishing Director

Editorial Directions, Inc.: E. Russell Primm, Editorial Director; Pam Rosenberg, Line Editor; Katie Marsico, Assistant Editor; Matthew Messbarger, Editorial Assistant; Susan Hindman, Copy Editor; Susan Ashley, Proofreader; Julie Zaveloff, Chris Simms, and Peter Garnham, Fact Checkers; Tim Griffin/IndexServ, Indexer; Dawn Friedman, Photo Researcher; Linda S. Koutris, Photo Selector

The Design Lab: Kathleen Petelinsek, Art Direction; Kari Thornborough, Page Production

*Photo*

Cover: Interior photographs: Cover: Bettmann/Corbis; New York Public Library/Art Resource, NY: 21; Bettmann/Corbis: 2; Owen Franken/Corbis: 27; Paul A. Souders/Corbis: 28; Hulton|Archive/ Getty Images: 10, 12, 18, 24; Time Life Pictures/Getty Images: 19; The Granger Collection, New York: 8, 22, 26; North Wind Picture Archives: 6, 9, 13, 14, 15, 16, 20, 23.

*Library of Congress Cataloging-in-Publication Data*

Burgan, Michael.
   John Paul Jones : naval hero / by Michael Burgan.
      v. cm. — (Our people)
   Includes bibliographical references (p.  ) and index.
   Contents: Early years at sea—From accused criminal to navy captain—The major battles—Last cruises.
   ISBN 1-59296-175-4 (alk. paper)
   1. Jones, John Paul, 1747–1792—Juvenile literature. 2. Admirals—United States—Biography—Juvenile literature. 3. United States. Navy—Biography—Juvenile literature. 4. United States—History—Revolution, 1775–1783—Naval operations—Juvenile literature. [1. Jones, John Paul, 1747–1792. 2. Admirals. 3. United States—History—Revolution, 1775–1783—Naval operations.] I. Title. II. Series.
   E207.J7B97 2004
   973.3'5'092—dc22                                      2003018121

12          20          24

# *Contents*

# Chapter ONE

# Early Years at Sea

*Thomas Jefferson once described John Paul Jones as "the principal hope of America's future efforts on the ocean."*

IN 1775, AMERICAN COLONISTS BEGAN A **REVOLUTION** to win their independence from Great Britain. Most of this war was fought on land, but some important battles took place at sea. One of the great naval heroes for the Americans was John Paul Jones. As captain of several different warships, Jones captured British vessels and raided enemy ports at a time when the Americans had not had other victories.

Jones was a brilliant captain and a brave fighter. At times, however, he got into trouble because of his temper. People who knew him thought he was only interested in winning fame and making money. But Jones insisted that he fought in the revolution to win Americans freedom.

John Paul Jones was born on July 6, 1747. His last name was actually Paul; he took the name Jones as an adult. His parents lived in Scotland near the town of Kirkcudbright. John's father was the gardener for a wealthy landowner. His mother worked as the landowner's housekeeper.

The Paul family home in Scotland was close to the seashore, and John often saw ships of all sizes sailing by. He enjoyed talking to sailors at the nearby port, and he played games in small rowboats with his friends. When John was about 13, his parents sent him to work for John Younger, owner of the vessel *Friendship.* This small ship carried goods between England and the colony of Virginia. Onboard the *Friendship,* John learned how to **navigate** and work the ship's sails.

In 1764, Younger sold the *Friendship.* Paul ended up on a ship that carried African slaves to British ports in the **West Indies.** He worked in the slave trade for several years, until he became disgusted with transporting slaves across the ocean. In 1768, he left a slave ship and boarded the *John,* a merchant ship heading to Scotland. Along the way, the captain and his assistant died from an illness. Paul took over as captain and safely sailed the vessel across the ocean. The owners of the *John* decided to make him the ship's new captain. Paul was just 21—a young age for a sailor to become master of a ship.

JOHN PAUL'S VOYAGES ON SLAVE SHIPS WERE PART OF WHAT IS KNOWN AS THE triangular trade. During colonial times, ships often sailed to three different ports on one trading voyage. A ship might carry food and other supplies from New England to British colonies in the West Indies. Then the ship took sugar and fruit from one of those colonies to England. On the last side of the "triangle," the ship carried English products such as clothes or tools back to New England.

Slaves were often the only cargo aboard a ship sailing from Africa to the British colonies in North America. A slave ship took rum and other products from New England to Africa. It then picked up slaves to bring them to the

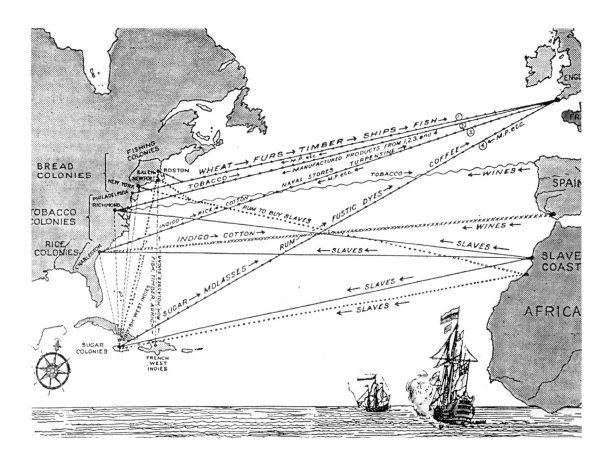

West Indies, New England, or the southern colonies in America. The voyage from Africa to North America was called the Middle Passage. The ship owners crowded the Africans below the ship's main deck, chaining them together two by two. Many slaves died along the way of starvation and sickness. After the slaves who survived the journey were sold off, the ship took molasses from the West Indies to New England, where it was made into rum. Many British and New England sea captains and ship owners made their fortunes on the slave trade.

# Chapter TWO

# From Accused Criminal to Navy Captain

*Today the cat o' nine tails would be considered a torture device but there was a time when it was a common tool used to punish people on ships for any number of reasons. Usually made of cow or horse hide, the whips often had steel balls or barbs of wire attached to the end of each tail.*

UNDER JOHN PAUL'S COMMAND, THE *JOHN* CARRIED a variety of goods between Scotland and the West Indies. Paul made the long voyage several times and always sailed his ship safely to shore. On one trip, however, Captain Paul's actions toward a crew member caused him some trouble.

The carpenter onboard the *John* was not very skilled at his craft, and he sometimes disobeyed Paul's orders. For punishment, the captain had the carpenter whipped. When the *John* reached port, the carpenter returned to Scotland on another ship, which arrived there before the *John* did. Along the way, the carpenter died of a fever. When his father heard about the beating his son had received under Captain Paul's orders, he

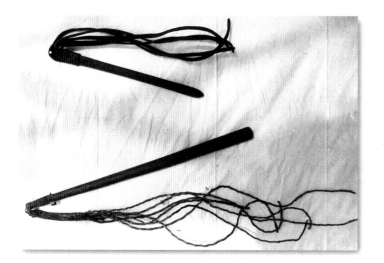

accused Paul of having murdered his son. Fortunately, Paul was able to prove in court that the man had died from sickness, not from the punishment he received on the *John.*

By 1772, Paul was captain of a larger merchant ship, the *Betsy.* His first voyage on the new vessel went well. But the second trip started off poorly and only got worse. As he wrote to a friend, the *Betsy* was "so very leaky that it was with the greatest difficulty that we could keep her free [of water] with both pumps." Paul had to pull into port and repair the ship. The *Betsy* finally reached the West Indies around October 1773.

On the island of Tobago, Paul ran into more trouble. Some of the crew demanded that he pay them in advance for some of their work. He refused, and the sailors tried to leave the ship without permission. A fight broke out, and Paul killed one of the crewmen with his sword. Paul's friends on Tobago convinced him that he would not get a fair trial there, even though he had acted in self-defense. Instead of risking a long jail sentence, he fled the island.

For almost two years, Paul kept moving. Historians are not sure how he spent his time as a fugitive. At one point in 1774, he landed in Virginia, and he may have spent time in North Carolina as well. During his travels, Paul changed his name, possibly to avoid being arrested for his actions in Tobago. For a time, he was known as John Jones,

11

*Minutemen battle the British at Lexington, Massachusetts, in the first battle of the Revolutionary War. The minutemen were members of the colony's militia—or armed forces— who agreed to be ready to fight at a minute's notice.*

then he chose the name he is known by today—John Paul Jones.

Sometime during the summer of 1775, Jones settled in Philadelphia, Pennsylvania. By this time, the American Revolution was under way. In April, British troops and local **militia** had battled in the Massachusetts towns of Lexington and Concord. Americans in the other colonies were coming to Massachusetts's aid. Colonial representatives met in Philadelphia at the Second Continental Congress. The members of Congress debated how to fight the British and gain American freedom.

Congress formed the Continental army and chose George Washington as its commander. The leaders also formed the Continental navy. In May 1776, Jones took command of his own ship, the

*Providence.* At the time, he was a first lieutenant, but within several months, John Hancock, president of the Continental Congress, signed Jones's promotion to captain. Throughout the rest of the year, Jones and his crew captured British merchant ships and their cargo and fought battles with British warships.

In September 1776, Jones boarded the *Alfred,* and led a small fleet of ships to Halifax, Nova Scotia. The fleet was on a mission to rescue American prisoners. The rescue failed because of bad weather and, as Jones sailed for the safety of Plymouth Harbor, he lost one ship to the British. Congress then had a new mission for Jones. Instead of sailing off the coast of North America, he crossed the Atlantic Ocean to fight the British in Europe.

## In CONGRESS.

The DELEGATES of the UNITED STATES of *New Hampshire, Massachusetts Bay Rhode-Island, Connecticut, New York, New-Jersey, Pennsylvania, Delaware, Maryland, Virginia North-Carolina, South-Carolina, and Georgia, TO*

*John Paul Jones, Esquire,*

WE, reposing especial Trust and Confidence in your Patriotism, Valour, Conduct and Fidelity DO, by these Presents, constitute and appoint you to be *Captain Navy* of the armed ———— called the ———— in the Service of the United States of North-America, fitted out for the Defence of American Liberty, and for repelling every hostile Invasion thereof. You are therefore carefully and diligently to discharge the Duty of *Captain* by doing and performing all manner of Things thereunto belonging. And we do strictly charge and require all Officers, Marines and Seamen under your Command, to be obedient to your Orders as *Captain* And you are to observe and follow such Orders and Directions from Time to Time as you shall receive from this or a future Congress of the United States, or Committee of Congress for that Purpose appointed, or Commander in Chief for the Time being of the Navy of the United States, or any other your superior Officer, according to the Rules and Discipline of War, the Usage of the Sea, and the Instructions herewith given you, in Pursuance of the Trust reposed in you. This Commission to continue in Force until revoked by this or a future Congress.

DATED at *Philadelphia October 10th 1776*

*By Order of the* CONGRESS,

*John Hancock*   PRESIDENT

*In 1776, John Hancock signed this order promoting John Paul Jones to the rank of captain.*

BEFORE THE AMERICAN REVOLUTION, THE 13 AMERICAN COLONIES RELIED ON British warships to guard their ports and protect merchant ships at sea. The war forced the colonies to assemble their own navy. During the summer of 1775, George Washington used a small fleet of armed merchant ships to capture British ships sailing near Boston. Later in the year, Congress began building an official American navy.

The first eight American ships were larger merchant vessels that carried from 6 to 30 cannons. At the time, the British had more than 2,000 warships in the Atlantic Ocean. Many of these carried 40 guns or more. On both sides, the cannons were classified by the weight of the cannonballs they fired. The largest guns in the early American fleet were nine-pounders. Some of the British guns were as large as 18 pounds.

During the war, the United States built a small fleet of new ships designed strictly for war. Three of these—the *Raleigh,* the *Ranger,* and the *America*—were built in Portsmouth, New Hampshire. John Paul Jones was in charge of getting all the necessary equipment and supplies for the ships and of gathering a crew.

To fight the British at sea, the United States also used privateers. These privately owned ships sailed for the U.S. government but were not part of the navy. They carried cannons, and their mission was to take British merchant ships as prizes. The privateers' owners and sailors made money by selling the goods aboard the ships they captured and by selling the ships for prize money.

# Chapter THREE

# The Major Battles

*Though Jones was hoping for a bigger and better warship, the* Ranger *proved to be adequate. On April 24th, Jones captured the British ship, the* Drake, *off the coast of Ireland. Jones then turned his attention to looting the British coast.*

LEAVING PORTSMOUTH, NEW HAMPSHIRE, ON THE **frigate** *Ranger* in early November 1777, Jones arrived in France in December. France and Great Britain were enemies, and the French were eager to help the Americans defeat the British. In France, Jones thought he was going to take command of a much larger warship. He learned, however, that the United

States could not afford to buy the new vessel he had been promised. Jones was stuck with the *Ranger,* which he thought was too small for the missions he hoped to carry out. Still, he and his crew prepared for action. Jones's plan was to raid the coast of Great Britain. He would attack ships, burn towns, and try to kidnap important British citizens.

In April 1778, Jones left France to cruise around the British Isles. Within a few days, he had taken his first prize ship. Jones then prepared for a land attack. The *Ranger* pulled into Whitehaven, England, a port Jones had sailed from when he was a teen. He led a raid on a British fort. As Jones later explained, the Americans did not have ladders, so they "climbed on the shoulder of the biggest . . . men and by this means we entered the fort." They placed spikes in the fort's cannons so they could not be fired. Jones and his men returned to the port to set fire to the ships there. But the Americans only torched one vessel before they were forced to flee.

The Whitehaven raid did not go as well as Jones had hoped. His plans to capture a local landowner also backfired. The man Jones hoped to take had left for his home in Scotland. Still, the British were shocked that their coast had been attacked.

The American captain had better luck a few weeks later, capturing a British warship. In May, the *Ranger* returned to France after taking seven prizes and capturing about 200 enemy sailors. This was a great success, the first for the new U.S. navy.

Jones still wanted a larger ship. It took him about six months to find *Le Duc de Duras,* a French ship that carried 40 guns. The vessel was twice as big as any ship Jones had commanded before. He renamed it *Bonhomme Richard,* in honor of Benjamin Franklin. One of the leaders of the American Revolution, Franklin published *Poor Richard's* **Almanac.** *Bonhomme Richard* is French for "good-hearted Richard."

In the summer of 1779, the *Bonhomme Richard* led a small **squadron** out of French waters. The other ships included the frigate *Alliance,* three smaller warships, and two French privateers. Jones sailed his ships around Great Britain, and by late September he had captured 17 prizes. British newspapers began calling him a pirate.

On September 23, Jones spotted a fleet of about 40 British merchant ships heading toward the coast of England. Protecting them were two warships, the *Serapis* and the *Countess of Scarborough.* Jones closed in on the fleet, while the

*When John Paul Jones needed a new ship, he asked Benjamin Franklin, the American ambassador to France at the time, to help him get one from the French. In August 1779, Franklin managed to get an old French ship for Jones who renamed the ship* Bonhomme Richard *to honor Franklin, one of his greatest heroes.*

John Paul Jones was celebrated by the Americans as a master commander of war ships. To the British, however, his looting and kidnapping plans made him as ruthless as a pirate.

captain of the *Serapis* prepared to defend the merchant ships.

As night fell, Jones and his crew began the most historic sea battle of the American Revolution. The *Bonhomme Richard* fired on the *Serapis,* which carried 50 guns. At almost the same moment, the British fired on Jones's ship. "The battle being thus begun," Jones later wrote, "was continuing with [unending] fury."

## Interesting Fact

The crew on the *Bonhomme Richard* included volunteers from Sweden, Portugal, Italy, Norway, and Switzerland.

19

*The* Serapis *was a faster, more easily maneuvered ship that carried much more artillery than the* Bonhomme Richard.

The battle started badly for the Americans. Two large cannons on the *Bonhomme Richard* exploded, and the ship took direct hits from the British cannons. Jones decided to bring his ship close to the *Serapis*. At close range, Jones's men could fire their guns at the enemy crew. The move to pull alongside the *Serapis* failed at first, and Jones tried again. Finally, the two ships were side by side.

The fighting continued for two hours. American **grenades** exploded on the *Serapis*, starting fires throughout the ship. Americans gunners shot

British sailors working on deck. Still, the British were able to keep firing their cannons, hitting Jones's vessel over and over again. At one point, the captain of the *Serapis* called out, asking Jones if he were ready to surrender. He replied defiantly that he had not even begun to fight!

The *Bonhomme Richard* was taking on water and seemed ready to sink. But by now, the *Serapis* was also badly damaged. The British had tried to board the American ship, but Jones's crew fought them off. Seeing that Jones would not surrender,

*Jones' victory over the* Serapis *and the immortal words "I have not yet begun to fight!" gave colonists newfound hope that freedom from British tyranny was possible.*

21

the British captain realized he could not go on. He surrendered to Jones. The Americans then took control of the *Serapis,* because their ship was about to sink. Jones sailed for Holland, commanding his greatest prize of the war.

*Jones captures the* Serapis. *This historic battle was the American navy's first defeat of a British ship in British waters.*

THE BATTLE BETWEEN THE *SERAPIS* AND THE *BONHOMME RICHARD* LASTED FOR about four hours. Jones should have received help from the other large warship in his squadron, the *Alliance* (below). Instead, the *Alliance's* cannons fired at the *Bonhomme Richard* several times during the battle. Jones later claimed these attacks were not an accident.

The captain of the *Alliance* was Pierre Landais. A French naval officer, Landais apparently did not like serving under Jones. According to some reports, he ordered his crew to shoot at the *Bonhomme Richard.* The cannon blasts damaged the ship and killed several crew members.

Jones was convinced Landais had tried to hit the American ship. No one is sure if Jones was right. One historian, however, agrees with him. Landais supposedly admitted later on that he had tried to destroy Jones's ship. He then planned to capture the *Serapis* himself so he could claim to be the winner of the battle. At the very least, Landais and the *Alliance* did not help the *Bonhomme Richard* during its battle.

Back on shore, Jones tried to have Landais removed from service. Landais managed to avoid a **court martial.** He kept sailing for the Americans until 1780, when he started showing signs of mental illness. This time, Landais was forced to leave the navy.

# Chapter FOUR

# Last Cruises

*Jones always thought of himself as a great champion of American liberty but he also intended to profit from his taking of enemy merchant ships as prizes. He found collecting his dues, though, to be difficult because of the strict policies of Congress about how prize money was distributed. Eventually he did receive a share of his money.*

FOR THE REST OF THE AMERICAN REVOLUTION, John Paul Jones did not see much naval action. He left Holland onboard the *Alliance,* which he sailed to Spain looking for prizes. He and his crew took just one British ship, then headed for France. In September 1780, Jones took command of the *Ariel* and sailed for the United States. Along the way, the ship attacked a British privateer. The enemy ship slipped away, however, before the Americans could claim it as a prize.

In February 1781, the *Ariel* reached Philadelphia. Congress praised Jones for his work in Europe, especially his victory over the *Serapis.* The lawmakers decided to name Jones captain of a new ship, the *America.* The ship, however, was still being built. Jones traveled to New Hampshire to supervise the vessel's construction.

The construction of the *America* took many months. Congress lacked money to spend on the ship. The builders also had trouble getting workers and supplies because the British were blockading American ports. Jones later wrote that getting the *America* built was "the most disagreeable service to which I was assigned during the whole course of the Revolution."

Then, before Jones could take the ship into battle, Congress took it away from him. The government gave the *America* to France, to replace a French ship that sank near Boston. Jones was deeply disappointed, but he did not complain.

For a few months, Jones sailed with a French fleet in the West Indies. By this time, the American Revolution was almost over. In the spring of 1783, Jones returned briefly to Philadelphia before leaving for France. He stayed in France for most of the next five years, though he made one voyage back to the United States in 1787.

In 1788, Jones agreed to command a fleet for Russia. During the 18th century, naval officers sometimes worked for other countries, if their homelands were not at war. Russian leaders made Jones a rear admiral, one of the highest ranks available. He served Russia for a little more than a year. During that time, he helped the Russians win several naval battles against Turkey.

When Jones left Russia, he traveled throughout Europe before finally settling in Paris, France. Poor and alone, Jones died there from a lung disease on July 18, 1792. He was buried in Paris, with only a few friends attending the funeral.

*Jones hoped that by going to Russia and commanding their naval fleet he would qualify for a more important title when the United States assembled a permanent navy.*

*John Paul Jones lived in this building in Paris, France. He died there on July 18, 1792.*

Over the years, Americans seemed to forget about John Paul Jones and his heroic actions. His gravesite in Paris was ignored. Then, at the end of the 19th century, Americans began to think about Jones again. In 1905, his grave was discovered.

## Interesting Fact

When Jones returned to the United States in 1787, Congress gave him a gold medal for his service during the American Revolution. He was the only person in the Continental navy to receive that honor.

Before he died, Jones did not know that he had been given one last chance to serve the United States. In June 1792, President George Washington named him a consul—someone who represents a country in foreign affairs. Jones was supposed to try to end a dispute between the United States and pirates based in Algeria. He died before news of the appointment reached him.

The U.S. government paid to have his body returned to the United States. Admiral Jones was carried across the Atlantic in a naval vessel and was buried in a richly decorated stone coffin in the crypt of the U.S. Naval Academy in Annapolis, Maryland. These words in the **crypt** describe the important role Jones played for his country: "He gave our navy its earliest traditions of heroism and victory."

*Though his death was not greeted with much fanfare, John Paul Jones was eventually given a hero's burial in the United States.*

28

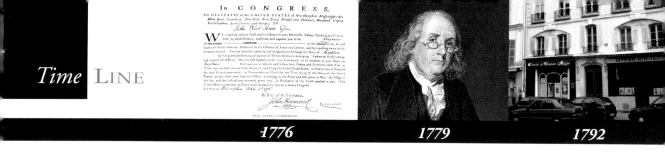

**1747** John Paul is born on July 6 near Kirkcudbright, Scotland.

**1760** Paul boards the *Friendship* as an apprentice sailor.

**1764** Paul ends his apprenticeship and begins serving on slave ships.

**1768** Returning to Scotland on the *John,* Paul takes over as captain.

**1773** Paul kills a crewman and flees the island of Tobago.

**1774** John Paul renames himself John Paul Jones; he travels to Virginia.

**1775** Jones is named a lieutenant in the Continental navy.

**1776** Jones is promoted to captain and commands the *Providence.*

**1777** Onboard the *Ranger,* Jones sails to Europe.

**1778** Jones leads a daring raid on Whitehaven, England.

**1779** Commanding the *Bonhomme Richard,* Jones captures the British warship *Serapis.*

**1781** Jones returns to the United States and supervises construction of his new ship, the *America.*

**1782** The U.S. government gives the *America* to France; Jones briefly sails with a French fleet in the West Indies.

**1783** Jones returns to Europe.

**1787** During a visit to America, Jones receives a gold medal from the U.S. Congress.

**1788** Jones serves as a rear admiral in the Russian Navy.

**1790** Jones settles in Paris, France.

**1792** Jones dies on July 18 in Paris.

**1905** Jones's grave is discovered, and the U.S. government brings his body back to America.

**almanac (AWL-muh-nak)**
An almanac is a yearly booklet with weather, astronomy, and other information. Ben Franklin's *Poor Richard's Almanac* was the best-known almanac in the American colonies.

**court martial (KORT MAR-shuhl)**
A court martial is a military trial to decide if a soldier or sailor disobeyed orders. Jones wanted Pierre Landais to face a court martial.

**crypt (KRIPT)**
A crypt is an underground room where people are sometimes buried. A crypt at the U.S. Naval Academy holds the body of John Paul Jones.

**frigate (FRIG-uht)**
A frigate is a type of warship with three masts and several dozen cannons. Frigates were the largest U.S. warships during the American Revolution.

**grenades (gruh-NADES)**
Grenades are small, hand-held explosives thrown at an enemy. Sailors once used grenades when fighting close to an enemy ship.

**militia (muh-LISH-uh)**
A militia is a group of citizens who serve as soldiers during an emergency. The United States used both the Continental army and state militias during the American Revolution.

**navigate (NAV-uh-gate)**
To navigate is to steer a ship from one point to the next. John Paul learned to navigate aboard the *Friendship.*

**revolution (rev-uh-LOO-shuhn)**
A revolution is a war fought by citizens against their rulers. John Paul Jones was a captain in the Continental navy during the American Revolution.

**squadron (SKWAHD-ruhn)**
A squadron is a group of ships that sail together. The squadron Jones commanded in 1779 had seven ships.

**West Indies (WEST IN-deez)**
The West Indies is a group of islands in the Caribbean Sea. Jones worked on a ship that carried African slaves to British ports in the West Indies.

# For Further INFORMATION

## Web Sites

Visit our home page for lots of links about John Paul Jones:
**http://www.childsworld.com/links.html**

*Note to Parents, Teachers, and Librarians:*
We routinely verify our Web links to make sure they're safe,
active sites—so encourage your readers to check them out!

## Books

Bradford, James C. *John Paul Jones and the American Navy.* New York: Power Plus Books, 2002.

Lutz, Norma Jean. *John Paul Jones: Father of the U.S. Navy.* Philadelphia: Chelsea House Publishers, 2000.

Simmons, Clara Ann. *John Paul Jones: America's Sailor.* Annapolis: Naval Institute Press, 1996.

## Places to Visit or Contact

**The Navy Museum**
*To learn more about the history of the U.S. Navy*
805 Kidder Breese SE
Washington Navy Yard
Washington, DC 20374-5060
202/433-4882

**The United States Naval Academy**
*To visit the crypt of John Paul Jones*
121 Blake Road
Annapolis, MD 21402-5000
410/263-6933

## About the Author

MICHAEL BURGAN IS A FREELANCE WRITER OF BOOKS FOR children and adults. A history graduate of the University of Connecticut, he has written more than 60 fiction and nonfiction children's books for various publishers. For adult audiences, he has written news articles, essays, and plays. Michael Burgan is a recipient of an Edpress Award and belongs to the Society of Children's Book Writers and Illustrators.